# Accompanying

## Young People on their Spiritual Quest

GS Misc 523

# Accompanying

## Young People on their Spiritual Quest

**Maxine Green and Chandu Christian**

CHURCH HOUSE
PUBLISHING

Church House Publishing
Church House
Great Smith Street
London SW1P 3NZ

ISBN 0 7151 4908 3

Published 1998 by the National Society and Church House Publishing
and on behalf of the Board of Education of the General Synod of the
Church of England

Third impression 2004

Cover design by ie Design, Birmingham

Printed in England by Biddles Ltd, King's Lynn

# Contents

# Foreword

We are becoming familiar with the theme 'accompanied journey'. The Emmaus story is a paradigm for such a journey. *Accompanying Young People on their Spiritual Quest* illuminates this theme richly and does so largely by telling stories.

The theology lies in the discovery that what we often think of as ordinary has a profound depth. The authors rightly say that 'the term accompanying is exceptionally hard to define although when people hear a few examples they click into the meaning of the term from their own experience'.

We shall find our own experiences of accompanying and being accompanied hugely enriched by this book.

✠    David Ripon
Chairman
General Synod Board of Education

# Acknowledgements

The authors appreciate and thank the Diocesan Youth Officer Network for their help and encouragement – especially Yvonne Criddle, Tony Williams and Katie Sparham who provided advice and discernment. They also wish to thank Pat Barton and Janice Overington of the National Youth Office for their excellent administrative support.

The authors are grateful to those people who have accompanied them in the past and accompany them in the present especially Raziya and Chris.

The authors and publisher gratefully acknowledge permission to reproduce copyright material in this book. Every effort has been made to trace and contact copyright holders. If there are any inadvertent omissions we apologise to those concerned and will ensure that a suitable acknowledgement is made at the next reprint.


Pages 2, 3, 6, 23-4, 59: Scriptures quoted from the *Good News Bible* published by the Bible Societies/HarperCollins Publishers Ltd UK © American Bible Society, 1966, 1971, 1976, 1992.

Page 16: Extract from T.S. Eliot, 'Little Gidding' in *Four Quartets* from *Collected Poems* 1909-1962, published by Faber and Faber and reproduced by permission of the publishers.

# 1

# Introduction

The idea for this book came via an unplanned route. Last September, the National Youth Officer for the Church of England, Maxine Green, and a number of Diocesan Youth Officers, Katie Sparham, Yvonne Criddle, Tony Williams and Chandu Christian, former Principal of the YMCA George Williams College, met to discuss the concept of mentoring and how best it could be explored further for the benefit of young people with whom we work. We revisited the Greek story which has given us the word 'mentoring'. The war between the Trojans and the Greeks is just about to begin. Odysseus, King of Ithaca, a great warrior and a highly rational person, is in turmoil about whether to join the war or to stay at home. The oracle has told him that if he does go to Troy, he will not return to Ithaca for twenty years. But he has a young son, the future king, who needs his father around him. So what should he do? The dilemma will not go unnoticed by many, many working parents, especially mothers, who feel torn between staying at home to be with their children and going to work. Eventually, Odysseus decides to join the war. He entrusts the care of his son Telemachus to his wise friend, Mentor. So it fell on Mentor to be the friendly adult on whom young Telemachus could rely. Such was the level of trust developed between the two that, when a deity wanted to help Telemachus at one stage, she took the form of Mentor, *and accompanied him on a journey*. When her job was done, she quietly disappeared.

Although the similarity between the Greek narrative and the New Testament narrative of the Road to Emmaus is quite striking, we were not aware of it at first. In fact we did not think of the New Testament story. We realized that we were using the word 'mentoring' in a very loose sense. We knew it was different from counselling, or supervision, but we could not create boundaries that would set mentoring apart from the other forms of helping processes. In the midst of our deliberations, Martin Cavender,[1] who had briefly joined our discussion,

---

[1] Martin Cavender works for Springboard, an initiative of the Archbishops of Canterbury and York for Evangelism.

suggested that we might look at the narrative of the road to Emmaus. As we began to reflect on the story, it seemed to us that here was a practice that was perhaps used in the Church but not widely acknowledged, where one person joins another just to be alongside them and 'join in' with whatever the first person wants to converse about. Maxine Green named this phenomenon 'accompanying'. She produced the example of a pianist preparing to accompany a soloist, or how a tabla (drum) player waits till the sitar player starts, and then picks up his or her pace, mood and tone, and then matches them on the tabla as an accompaniment. She shares this analogy in greater detail in Chapter 3. We also came across the work of Lister Tonge[2] with Llysfasi Spirituality Course,[3] which he defines as a 'programme for those seeking to know more about accompanying the faith/life journey of others'. As this information began to merge with our fresh discoveries about the road to Emmaus, we all felt that accompanying was definitely a laudable practice, based on the principles that were contained within the story of Emmaus. We felt that rather than follow our original aims of exploring mentoring, we should endeavour to bring into focus our new understandings and insights. Consulting the *Shorter Oxford Dictionary*, we saw that 'accompanying' was formed from *com* meaning 'together with' and *panis* meaning 'bread'. The original meaning was 'any relish such as meat or cheese eaten with bread'. Thus a companion is someone who acts as a relish on our journey, making it more enjoyable. Our desire to explore the concept of accompanying became stronger with this discovery. We revisited the road to Emmaus narrative (Luke 24.13-35). With a mental picture of the two people from Emmaus eating *panis*, bread, with Jesus, the actual and the metaphorical images of accompaniment merged in our minds. Here were two people eating bread with some relish, perhaps cheese; here were also two people with a stranger who accompanied them, acting as a relish on their journey, enabling them to move from their state of despair and confusion to where they felt a 'fire burning in us' (Luke 24.32). We were now more keen and more determined to explore the concept of accompanying. This book is an outcome of that 'fire' that began to burn within us.

---

[2] Lister Tonge is Chaplain to the Community of St John the Baptist, Clewer, Windsor.

[3] Llysfasi Spirituality Course, Isabel Gregory, 60 St Mary's Road, Liverpool L36 5ST.

## The aim of this book

From the outset, we knew that we did not want the book to be a theological tome. Nor did we want it to be a manual of 'How to', or 'Ten Tips on Being a Relish'! We wanted it to be a book that would give readers some insights into the activity of accompanying and at the same time leave them free to make their own discoveries, from their past, for the future practice of accompanying. We wanted to outline the qualities that we saw as important, but at the same time did not want them to appear as a kind of 'person specification' of essential attributes. Our thinking behind this was that whilst it is useful to outline the helpful attributes of a job, there are countless examples in the Bible where God has enabled people to accompany others in their hour of need. The mission of accompanying starts in the Bible soon after the creation of Adam, when God says: 'I will make a suitable companion to help him' (Genesis 2.18). In the New Testament, Paul, although a prisoner on a boat caught in a stormy sea, acts as a great companion:

> 'Not even a hair of your heads will be lost.' After saying this, Paul took some bread, gave thanks to God before them all, broke it, and began to eat. They took heart, and every one of them also ate some food.
>
> (Acts 27.34-6)

This happens, thanks to Paul's reassuring accompaniment, after fourteen days of not eating out of fear! Thus we see accompanying more as a Christian way of life which can be practised in any situation, rather than a professional practice worthy of a National Vocational Qualification.

There are countless examples of accompanying in everyday, ordinary life. A parent who accompanies a child venturing out on his or her first newspaper round on a dark morning, a friend who accompanies an unwell person to hospital, a church member who deliberately 'falls in' with a newer member of the church at a coffee morning, are all examples of accompanying. What we discovered in our explorations was that accompanying was more a state of mind than a set of skills. It was the ability to give the other person the same assurance that Jesus gave more than once: 'I am with you'. The Chinese character for the word 'listen' sums up our feeling about what accompanying involves. It is made of five symbols: ear, eye, you, heart and undivided attention. All these elements are seen as working together to form the word 'listen'. The other English parallels that we could think of were the statements: 'I am all ears', 'I am all eyes', 'I am whole-heartedly with you'. As a logo for accompanying, we could hardly do better than to adopt the Chinese character for 'listen'.

Once we opened up our minds, we were deeply influenced by the road to Emmaus narrative in the Gospels. We noticed that Jesus almost 'inserted' himself along with the two people walking back home. There was no effort, no deliberate drawing of attention to him; in fact he kept himself a stranger to them, despite the fact that they knew of him. He kept their pace, he talked their talk and he went in the direction they were going. He seemed to have no agenda of his own. Like a tabla player with a sitar player, he engaged in the conversation that was going on and made no effort to force its pace or content, and yet there is little doubt that his influence was felt, for the travellers felt comforted and inspired by what he said.

Regardless of whether he was hungry or not, he even waited till they reached their destination and offered him food. Then he accepted it, but as soon as their focus shifted on to him, he disappeared as effortlessly as he had joined them. This seems to us an important point: as soon as there is a possibility of the centre of attention shifting on to the accompanist, it is time to go.

Theodore Zeldin, in his series of talks on conversation, makes the point that conversations change the world. As we talk, we influence and are influenced by the conversation. Implicitly, Jesus makes the same point through his work on the road to Emmaus. The level of intimacy that was struck up between the stranger and the travellers can easily be seen from the fact that Jesus was invited to stay on for dinner. As they began the meal, Jesus engaged in a different conversation, this time with God, to thank him for the food. That is when the 'penny dropped' and the minds met. It is this 'meeting of minds' as Zeldin calls it which has the power to change the way we perceive the world. 'When minds meet, they don't just exchange facts: they transform them, reshape them, draw different implications from them, engage in new trains of thought. Conversation doesn't just reshuffle the cards: it creates new cards' (Zeldin 1998). Accompanying, we are saying (and Zeldin seems to concur), is a very powerful tool, as Jesus showed. It has the power to alter the way we feel, and the way we see the world.

If accompanying has the power to change the way we feel, as it did on the road to Emmaus, then it is bound to have not only spiritual, inner implications, but also social and political implications. Its dynamics could, according to Zeldin, produce far-reaching consequences. However, it is important to realize that for the accompanist, the process of accompanying is an end in itself. It is not done in order to produce some future outcome. In other words, it is not about *becoming* in the future; it is about *being* in the present, recognizing, relishing and living in the 'here and now', as it happens. Whenever it happens it has its own virtue, its own validity. It does not have to be towards some future end.

It is not possible to grasp the idea of accompanying as a stark and rigid concept. We are reminded of the story of three blindfolded people standing around an elephant – each one was asked to describe it. The first, who was holding the trunk, said that it was long and rough and seemed to be hollow. The second, holding the tail, said that it was whiskery, thin and solid, whilst the third described a massive roundness, the top of which he could not reach. Each view was right, but each was partial. Our aim in the book is to give you different views of accompanying, so that in your own mind you can build up a composite picture and know something of the whole. When you read the book you will notice changes in style; this is because while Chandu and Maxine agree and own all the words in the book, they have written individual chapters. We hope that this change of pace and style will enhance the reading and provide a suitable relish. The following chapters each have different pictures and approaches to offer.

## Spirit in young people

In this chapter, we focus especially on the way the Church can accompany young people on their spiritual road. It suggests that young people are not in 'deficit'. They already have the Spirit of God in them. It mainly draws on the parable of the Prodigal Son to derive some insights about 'accompanying' young people in a variety of ways.

5

## Accompanying

In this chapter, we offer some of our insights about the concept and practice of accompanying. We outline some of the ingredients of accompanying. We also try to define what it is not. We suggest how someone may choose an accompanist if they so wish. We offer some examples of accompanying from a variety of sources. This is where we try to separate the process of accompanying from that of counselling or from other, similar processes. We show in particular that it is not a skill, but rather a way of being. We introduce the notion of peer accompaniment and suggest the advantages it has. Throughout the book we are at pains not to turn accompaniment into another discipline or profession, however, we are aware that there are rules and regulations that particularly an adult wanting to accompany a young person must observe.

## Examples

When we let it be known that we were looking for case studies about accompanying, people sent in several examples. In this chapter, we have given a small sample of people's experiences. To retain confidentiality, we have disguised locations and changed names, but the details are factual in essence. The evidence that we gathered from the case studies is that accompanying is indeed a phenomenon that is practised at all age levels and in a variety of situations. In one episode, we saw young people accompanying an adult in return for the accompanying she had done for them.

## Further thoughts on developing accompanying

This chapter tries to sum up how we view accompanying as a phenomenon. We emphasize the importance of the past by inviting readers to reflect on their experiences. We suggest that the readers create a link between the two sides of accompaniment – times when they were accompanied, and times when they accompanied others. This, it seems to us, is the best way of learning about accompaniment, because, as we said earlier in the book, there is no planned curriculum for this practice, no National Vocational Qualification. We also acknowledge the need of an accompanist who himself or herself might feel the need of some support. We suggest that it should be possible for an accompanist to find an accompanist for their own needs, in the same way that Jesus, the accompanist, asked the disciples to keep him company in Gethsemane: 'The sorrow in my heart is so great that it almost crushes me. Stay here.' (Mark 14.34).

## Conclusion

What of the future? We have endeavoured to understand and celebrate the marvellous gift Jesus has given us by his work on the road to Emmaus, so simple and yet so powerful as to change the way people felt and thought about themselves and the world around them. We hope churches will consciously take on accompanying, just as Jesus did, as part of their agenda of action, and appreciate the great gift of being in the here and now. We do much work about the future, about becoming, but accompanying also gives us a unique opportunity to *be* the kingdom of God now. Accompanying is one of the most powerful manifestations of the divine statement: 'I am with you' – now.

We want the book to be an example of what it talks about. We want it to be a companion. We want it to be a tool that people can use as an accompaniment in itself. We want people to experience the essence of accompanying in all of their relationships with young people, so that grandparents, godparents, parents, teachers, priests, friends and anyone whose life touches young people will recognize and develop accompanying as part of these relationships. If this happens then we shall feel satisfied that we did the job we set out to do. We hope that you, the reader, will enjoy what follows in the rest of the book.

# 2

# Spirit in young people

## What do we mean by spirituality?

A newsletter from a branch of Youth for Christ (YFC) shows once again that young people have a deep interest in things supernatural. In its local survey, YFC also found that fewer young people considered themselves atheists than their counterparts did a few years ago.

We hope we are not 'bending' the report too far to suit our own purposes when we claim that the young people's interest in what the report called the 'supernatural' could well be a quest for understanding spirituality, that supernatural force within us. But what do we mean by spirituality? As Christians, we have a particular way of understanding spirituality that is so vividly depicted in the Bible. God creates a statue from clay, but it remains a statue, incapable of feeling, thinking, moving, or making decisions. All these capacities do not follow until God breathes the breath of life into it. The Latin word for breath is *spiritus* and that, according to the story, is what we received from God – his spirit – to become humans. In a very simple way, the story connects us with God. Without his spirit, his breath, working within us, we would be statues. The attribute of spirituality, of life, is what we are endowed with as a gift from God at the point of our creation.

But gifts often come wrapped, boxed and in a kit form, and before we can use them, we have to unwrap them, take them out of the box and assemble them. We think of the gift of spirituality like that. It is within us, but we do need to bring it out of its box and assemble it so that we can use it, experience it and enjoy it. When we are young and inexperienced, it is not always easy to open our gifts or to assemble them ourselves and we need a helping hand from someone who, though recognizing that it is our gift, helps us to unpack and assemble it and then leaves us alone to enjoy it. That is how God acts in the story of creation after he gives us his gift of spirit. He puts us in charge (Genesis 1.28).

The ability to awaken the spirit in others features often in the Old Testament and the New Testament. Take the story of Samuel (1 Samuel 3). Here is a young lad, already apprenticed to the Temple. He carries out the daily chores and he learns a few skills until the time comes when he feels an awakening within him. Most of us have experienced it, the restlessness, the confusion and the inability to make sense of all within our head. Does this not sound similar to the story of creation? In the beginning there is the chaos, the darkness, the void. Nothing makes sense. Then the spirit of the Lord moves across the 'raging ocean' (Good News version), and slowly everything begins to make sense. Now light is separated from darkness, sky from earth, water from land.

In Samuel's story, perhaps similar darkness and confusion prevail inside him, like a raging ocean, keeping him awake in the middle of the night, and he does not know what to do. Until, that is, Eli understands what is going on and helps Samuel see a way forward. Metaphorically speaking, this is the second birth, when a person with the help of an institution like the Church begins to lead a life that is fuller and richer, and is aware of the supernatural, something that is far above the natural and the visible. Moses was much older when his spirit awakened inside him, but his experience is not very different from that of Samuel's. Samuel hears a voice that he needs to fathom. Moses on the other hand sees an image and hears a voice that he needs to make sense of. When they experience this awakening, both of them are lifted from an ordinary life into one that is richer, more rewarding, fulfilling – and demanding.

## The role of the Church

If we relate these stories to the young people we see in our churches, or the ones that we would like to see in our churches, then the task of the adults in the Church becomes a little clearer. The adults could be members of the Parish Council, or the Youth Committee, or they could be Sunday School teachers. They could be adult worshippers in a church with a concern for young people. Whatever their station in the Church, there are at least two ways in which adults could help young people discover their spirit. One is to create the right environment in the Church in which the inquiring mind of the young people can be nourished. The other is to be like Eli, ready and patient to talk with them and to point them in the right direction for their spiritual fulfilment. How can this be done? We believe that this is where the concept and practice of accompanying comes into play. There must be multitudinous ways in which adults can 'accompany' a young person on his or her 'journey', be it an inner one or an outer one. Some people carry out this role imaginatively, others may need a little help. Here is an example, though it does not come from Church youth work.

A youth worker took a group of ten boys, aged 14 and 15, for a walk in Derbyshire. He knew the country well and planned the route with great care. He took the view that few young people actually enjoy walking for its own sake and therefore the journey had to be interspersed with a number of activities and incidents.

The group was shown the route on a map, and someone was elected to find the route for the first part of the way. Everybody took a turn at this. After a mile or two the group went through an old railway tunnel, stopping at the centre point where it was not possible to see the light from either end. There was a good deal of clowning about in the total darkness. A little later the group stopped by a dew pond and the response to the question 'How long do we stay here?' was 'five minutes or until the first one falls in'. Nobody did. A second stop was taken by some large boulders where the youth worker (himself an experienced climber) encouraged the young people to try their hand at rock climbing. The group worked strenuously at this, tackling more and more difficult problems, but never more than two or three feet from the ground. The youth worker taught without appearing to do so, making suggestions rather than giving instructions, encouraging and joking while ensuring that everybody had some degree of success. Lunch was taken by a limestone outcrop. After lunch the youth worker took out a geological hammer from his rucksack and chipped away at some pieces of rock. Asked what he was doing, he responded, 'go away, I'm busy'. Within ten minutes everyone was hunting for fossils and talking about them. The youth worker talked about the geological development of the area, expressing his detailed knowledge of the subject in simple and dramatic language. The afternoon stop was taken by a stream and the youth worker encouraged the group to take off their boots and socks and paddle. No one had done this in a mountain stream before. The final stage of the walk included a sunset and a view – and the route had been chosen with this in mind.

(HMI report, 1987)

The example shows how adults can turn an ordinary event into one that will make young people wonder about the world present and past. The youth worker accompanies young people and takes them out to see the world as it is. They experience the darkness of the tunnel, the coolness of the water and, indeed, the pleasure of the company of one another. They experience the world of the past, several million years old, as they begin to look for the fossils. It would not be too difficult to imagine that this experience would have led some to think about the creation of the universe. How was it made? Who made it? Before we know, they would be wondering and hearing voices. That is when they will need someone's company to help them come through the dark tunnel and see light at the other end.

## Our perception of young people

One of the problems that we adults face in working with young people is that, quite often, we are more organization-minded than we realize. The Church is both a movement and an organization. It is a movement because we are constantly on the move, seeking to reinterpret God's wishes and commands and learning to give up the old ways and adopting new ones. All the apostles had to learn this as they accepted the call to follow Jesus. Until Paul appeared on the scene, the Gentiles were out of the Church. Then they were in. Until fifty or even fifteen years ago, the role of women was perceived differently in the Church from the way it is today. It is one of the greatest strengths of Christianity that it remains a moving religion; its thinking and its practices remain open to question and open to change. But a movement, even a movement as strong as Moses' migrating Hebrews, has to have some organization. That particular movement starts with the ten commandments from God, but ends up with six hundred further rules! Of course we need rules, structures and roles, but they tend to turn a fluid, flexible movement into an organization with rigid boundaries and procedures. The process of organization begins as a *means* to facilitate the movement, just as the Mosaic laws were meant to facilitate the movement. However, more often than not, the organization begins to take over the movement *for its own sake*. Why is this so? Social psychologists tell us that all organizations tend to become more complex with the passage of time (Kast and Rosenzweig, 1985, p.107). It is therefore understandable if the Church as an organization creates a complex system which begins to have dominance over the less structured, more flexible side of the Church as a movement. We can now see perhaps a crude division between adults and young people in the Church. Adults, steeped in the ways of an organization, like to maintain it through their committees, rules and regulations. On the other hand, young people may represent the movement aspect of the Church and may not have much patience for rules and regulations. Adults like to use them, young people may want to replace or even discard them. (We are aware that the distinction we have drawn between young people and adults is a crude one, and in reality, the lines of division between the two groups are not as firmly drawn as our statement suggests.)

In the late fifties, William Whyte published a book called the *Organisation Man*, which showed us how individuals have become organization-minded and have acquired a kind of corporate identity which Whyte named the 'organisation man'. We could modify his insights and apply them to the Church as an organization and see that we might have created a similar identity for the Church whom we might call the 'Church person'. As a 'Church person', we may exert covert, and sometimes overt, pressure on young people to align themselves with this identity. We expect them to sit through the church services. We expect them to take on duties of various kinds. But, whereas William Whyte's organization man had accepted the organization's expectations of him, young people in the Church do not necessarily accept the Church person's expectations of them. They protest, they object, they vote with their feet and do not join the Church. How can we retain our spirit as a movement and enable our young people to discover their spirit, their God-given gift? What help does the Bible give us to understand this phenomenon?

We think this is where the notion of a journey, and the theme of this book, accompanying, come together. A movement by definition would be on a move, on a journey. A journey is often a vehicle by which people discover themselves. When young people go on a journey to discover themselves, we could be of help to them if we could accompany them, sometimes physically, sometimes in spirit.

## The parable of the Prodigal Son

The parable of the Prodigal Son (Luke 15.11-32) gives us quite a few insights about how young people might set off on a journey, full of unknown perils. It also shows us how we could help them discover their spirit. Quite often they are restless in the same way as Samuel was and seek a quick fix for their restlessness, in the way that the Prodigal Son did. Organizations, be they informal ones like a family or a formal one like a church, find it difficult to allow young people to stretch the boundaries of their being. So the youth go away, away from home, away from the Church. They have abundant energy, they can burn the candle at both ends, sometimes to the annoyance of adults. Grown-ups feel that they have a duty to restrain young people from making mistakes, from wasting energy and resources. They are not allowed to make mistakes, and yet mistakes are the engines for growth and development as we can see so clearly from the story of the Prodigal Son. It helps us to see what we as a Church need to do.

We should give to young people what belongs to them. The Church and the adults who comprise it are stewards rather than owners of all that they save, preserve and protect. The Church, its structures and its activities should all be in that category. So when young people come along and demand a portion of these as their own, we have to accept the claim and part with our cherished traditions, our rules and our control. It is only by doing so that we shall help young people to learn the responsibilities of ownership. This does not imply that we give up everything with abandon. Our responsibility as stewards is ongoing and we need to think of those who might not be vociferous in their claims.

We should part with our control without bitterness or condemnation, without a sense of loss, and with an understanding that giving away life or things is the only way to retain them in *essence*. We should then live, every day of our life, in the hope of a reunion, of reconciliation with our young people. When they do come back with their spirit awakened in them, we rejoice; we do not harp back on the past but look forward to that which we have regained and start a new, richer relationship.

## The deficit model of young people

What makes it difficult for us at times to follow the concepts from the story is that, almost unconsciously, we follow what Paulo Freire (1995) calls the 'banking concept' in our dealings with young people. We behave as if we are bank managers and young people are seeking a loan from us. We feel as if we own the money, and we want to be sure that our money will not be squandered if we lend it to them. We feel we have the answers and young people's questions are treated as a sign of deficit. This misunderstanding arises from the feeling that we own the bank rather than that we are merely stewards of it. We value answers more than we do questions, forgetting that it is the questions that lead to answers. Missing what the story teaches us, we lack the insight and the trust in young people to believe that, in the long run, what they may be struggling with is that awakening of the spirit rather than the short term self-indulgence. We only notice the self-indulgence and feel compelled to exercise our power and control, and yet countless real-life experiences tell us that such control frequently ends in disasters.

Carl Rogers, author and counsellor, devised another image which makes a similar point (Rogers, 1961). He said we tend to see young people as empty 'mugs' and ourselves as 'jugs', full of wisdom and knowledge. We 'pour out' a portion into the mugs as we think appropriate. Both Freire's and Rogers' images make the same point: young people are not empty vessels. When God created human beings, he blew his own spirit into them, so young people are filled with his spirit; they are not empty jugs or broke loan-seekers. God's exhortation is that we should not stop them from reaching out to him *now*. Theirs is the kingdom in heaven, in future, but they must not be stopped from reaching out to him *now*, in the present.

One way in which young people learn about how we treat them as empty mugs is the way their questions and answers are treated with a

14

certain amount of amusement by the grown-ups in a church service. Their views are treated as cute, but not as serious. It is not surprising that many young people, when they become aware of this phenomenon, refuse to participate in a question–answer session in a church service. Often their attempts to participate in adult activities are treated with similar condescension. Here is an example of what we mean.

From a very early age, Andrew would get up on a Sunday morning, eager to go to church. It was his job to give out the books at the door as people arrived and he was there every week with a smile. He was 7 or 8 years old but did a good job and it made him feel part of the church.

One Sunday, to his surprise, he found that a stranger was doing his job. Apparently he had fallen on hard times and the church wanted to make him feel welcome so they gave him Andrew's job. A few weeks later, the vicar asked for people to put their names down to act as sidespersons. Andrew put his name down. At the next PCC meeting, it was revealed that Andrew's was the only name on the list. This caused hilarity in the meeting. Andrew was not even thanked for his offer.

When we refuse to take young people seriously, we adults lose out and get accused of practising tokenism. What is worse, young people become full of apathy. Unfortunately, we see the cause of it lying within young people rather than seeing our contribution in creating it.

### What steps can we take to remedy this?

Despite our shortcomings as adults, we have a genuine concern for young people. One of the ways in which we can help them is to offer ourselves as role models. Role-modelling has been a buzz word since the eighties. For example, it is said that we need male role models in nursery and infant schools so that from a very young age, children can learn to imitate them. Imitation is a proven way of learning, both in the animal kingdom and in the human world. We can benefit in the Church from this way of learning. We can, for example, adopt the role model that the father in the story of the Prodigal Son provides. So what does the father's role teach us?

Before answering that question, it might be useful to remind ourselves of some of the traits that young people depict. First of all, they will learn by trial and error. They will leave home or church, they may squander away their wealth and they will experiment with relationships. They will make mistakes, and, if we have sustained our relationship with them, they will have a chance to learn from their errors. (The actor Stephen Fry, when he was a youth, took his father's credit card and blew several thousand pounds on it. But his parents welcomed him back. Today, he says: 'I recommend to every youngster to get a good set of parents!')

Secondly, we have to remember that the spirit – God's spirit – is already in them and that they *can* and almost certainly *will* acknowledge what is happening to them and seek help if they are not made to feel ashamed or unloved.

Finally, in some ways, young people have to go through the 'pigsty' experience where all is chaos and confusion. We are back to the story of creation. It is only by experiencing the chaos and darkness of the raging ocean that we can learn to let our spirit dance across the waters and separate the good from the bad. T.S. Eliot's lines, quoted below, have a resonance with the story of creation. It is only by completing our journey and coming back to our starting place that we know the true beginning. That is almost certainly what happened to the Prodigal Son.

> We shall not cease from exploration
>
> And at the end of all our exploring
>
> Will be to arrive where we started
>
> And know the place for the first time

> (T.S. Eliot, 'Little Gidding', part 5, 1969 )

### Insights from the father's role
We now return to the role of the father in the story and see what it has to offer us as a model. The first point is a reminder of what has already

been said before. We need to be prepared to hand over that for which we are only custodians. It could be material wealth or it could be freedom, but we need to be prepared to release our control of them, because they were not ours in the first place.

Secondly, we need to be prepared to wait. It may be some time before young people are ready to come back. We have to have enough trust in young people that they will return. Obviously, neither side will have that trust if we have not built it up over the years. Trust and faith go hand in hand. We saw a definition of faith on a poster which summed it up for us: 'Faith is what you have when you have nothing else to hang on to.' When we have evidence to hang on to, faith is not required. Faith thus has a spiritual quality in itself. It lies hidden within us, with our spirit. It is what we have as that inner voice or that inner image. It is not available to the scrutiny of our five senses, but it is something that we can hang on to, as Samuel and Moses did after their spiritual awakening. The father in the story never doubted that the son would return. He looked out for him every day. The combination of trust and faith sustained him through his pain and moments of weakness.

Thirdly, he was prepared for the son's return. He was not living merely in a fantasy world. He continued to work and prepare for what he would do when the son returned – lay on the best food, dress him in the best clothes and throw a party for everyone. No recrimination, no harping back to the past, but a new relationship based on a new discovery of love and bond between the two.

Fourthly, the father ran up to the son as soon as he caught sight of him, whilst he was still a long way off. We too need to develop a keen eye for a lookout and be prepared to go a long way to meet young people. For a short story, it gives us an amazing wealth of information about how to conduct ourselves with young people.

The story may give us what the psychologists call a mental map, a picture of the right attitudes, but we also need the skills to create the appropriate environment in which we can engage with young people. We have already seen an example of how one youth worker created this environment. We share more examples with the readers elsewhere in the book.

Each of these examples shows how different churches in different settings have tried to enable young people to discover the spirituality, the breath of God, within them. We need to remember that our own spirituality may also need sustaining from time to time – Jesus himself taught us that. At times we may have to pray or work so hard at it that our sweat might turn into blood. We need a total commitment to this mission, in the way that Elisha demonstrated when he was summoned to the house of a boy who had died (2 Kings 4.18-37).

Elisha refused to accept the finality of that situation. He put the boy on the floor, in the spreadeagle position. Then he lay down on the boy, putting his hands and legs and mouth on the boy. He was at one with the boy. It was as if his existence and that of the boy had merged into one. He then opened the mouth of the boy and blew his own breath. He blew his own breath into the mouth of the boy. That is what we too have to do – give our own breath in a situation where the breath might have temporarily gone out. God gave us his breath, our spirit. Elisha has shown us what we can do with it.

In this chapter, we have argued that spirituality is the very essence of life which God himself has endowed on human beings. As a result of that position, we have further argued that young people already come endowed with spirituality, but that as adults we may need to support them in their search for it when they feel a little lost. We have taken the example of the parable of the Prodigal Son as our main model to high-light some of the ways in which we can think about our responsibilities. There are some examples of good practice which have been included to provide models.

## Accompanying

What is the binding factor in our endeavour to enable young people to discover their spirituality? We think it is the process of accompanying, a concept which the rest of the book develops more specifically. The story of what Jesus did on the road to Emmaus recurs in the Bible with different characters, time, space and slant. Frequently we hear about the spirit of the Lord coming upon or being with a person. We hear about God walking in the Garden of Eden and then talking to Adam and Eve. We hear about God wrestling with Jacob all night. We hear about Eli and Samuel, Philip and the Ethiopian official, Saul (Paul) and Ananias. In today's world we can accompany people by a variety of means, by letters, telephones and electronic means. In the ancient world of the Prodigal Son, these different means might not have been available, but, nonetheless, the father waited eagerly for his son's return. One might enter a realm of fantasy here and say that somehow the son knew that the father would break the bread with him one day. That is what accompanying is about, just *being* there for the people who need us.

# 3

# The art of accompanying

## Painting the picture

Picture a pianist sitting at the piano, music in front of them, thinking ahead of how they are going to accompany the soloist who is about to perform. There is a level of concentration and attention as the accompanist tries to 'pick up' the mood and wishes of the soloist. There is sensitivity and awareness as the piece starts, and the accompanist gives a musical base and outline which the soloist can use as a spring-board for the performance.

This is accompanying, providing a framework, a safe base which the accompanied can use to explore different themes in their lives. A good accompanist is sensitive, attentive and knows that the creative energy to explore these themes comes from the accompanied themselves. An accompanist listens and is alert to those themes which are hidden and obscured and gently provides a framework and space where the accompanied can reveal and explore these for their growth and development.

> In 1996 the bottom fell out of my world. My parents were getting divorced, I was taking my A levels and I had a major row with my boyfriend. Everything I touched seemed fated to fall apart. I spent more and more time with Hannah. I would drop in after school and have a cup of tea and a chat. It wasn't so much what she *did*, it was more who she *was*. If she hadn't given me that time and space I know my life would have fallen apart and I'd never be here at university studying.

Accompanying occurs between all ages at any time, but the focus of this book is how young people can be accompanied as they move from being children to being adults.

## Accompanying as a gift

The greatest gift that we can give is to 'be alongside' another person. It is in times of crisis or achievement or when we have to manage long-term difficulties that we appreciate the depth and quality of having another person to accompany us. In Western society at the end of the twentieth century this gift has a fairly low profile. Although it is pivotal in establishing good communities its development is often left to chance and given a minor status compared with such things as management structure and formal procedures. It is our opinion that the availability of this sort of quality companionship and support is vital for people to establish and maintain their physical, mental and spiritual health and creativity. The purpose of this chapter is to explore what is happening in such a relationship so that we can identify and understand the process. We can then build on existing patterns of 'being alongside', particularly in our relationships with young people, and aim to develop new skills and deeper knowledge.

> Over the years of being a youth worker you begin to notice some individuals who are a bit lost with no one to talk to. If you hang around and make yourself available these folk tend to find their way to you. In my experience they do not want advice, they certainly don't want a lecture. They simply want to talk things through, or be silent, or walk, and when I manage to be patient and provide this space I look on as these young people gently unravel their problems in front of me. Afterwards they may thank me or just move on, and when they do I don't really know what I have done.

## What is accompanying?

We have had a real difficulty in trying to find the right words to describe this process of 'being there' for another person. In numerous conversations we would start to explain the help, support, hope and space we had received when we needed it and immediately the other person would understand what was meant. It is not the concept that is difficult; everyone we talked with had experienced this to some degree, at some point in his or her life. The problem was that there were no words that adequately described being given space, time, support and hope. This gift was especially appreciated during times of stress, growth, change and personal need.

Accompanying also takes the risk of rejection, and the risk of observing the lives of others and offering to listen and be there. It is especially valuable that this offer is available to young people who are experiencing times of change and transition in adolescence. At this time, when there is a search for identity and meaning young people, especially benefit from having space to explore and restore themselves through the accompanying relationship.

> I was a child of a vicarage who did everything everyone expected of me. I accepted the evangelical enthusiastic Christianity of my home and church as my own. When I went to college I suddenly saw life another way – I began to question my sexuality and my faith was crumbling. I needed to talk this through and phoned Jenny, who was a person I'd met from time to time at diocesan events, and asked if I could see her. It was a relief to be able to explain the way that my faith was being shaken and express my fears about being homosexual. She didn't answer my questions, she just let me ask them in the open and answer them myself. At the end of the conversation I hadn't set new things to do or come to any decisions, but I felt as if there had been some healing deep inside.

The term 'accompanying' is exceptionally difficult to define, although when people hear a few examples they click into the meaning of the term from their own experience. The way we will be explaining accompanying is by giving different pictures and stories which illuminate the accompanying relationship.

The central illustration is where accompanying relates to music, where the accompanist provides a musical framework which the soloist uses to explore the range of their instrument or voice. Music is made when there is an awareness between the two players, an empathy, so that the soloist can use the musical base confidently to attempt new variations of colour and tone in their instrumental performance.

In Indian music the accompanist plays a drum called a tabla. The tabla player starts drumming and as the beat and the pattern develop the sitar player joins in and improvises. Alternatively, the tabla player waits on the notes of the sitar, and listens carefully to detect the mood, direction and the pace and then picks this up and maintains the same tempo, keeping this until the sitar player changes their rhythm. The tabla player accompanies by giving a base percussion which gives energy to the sitar player and is the rhythm keeper, maintaining a musical heartbeat so that the sitar player may be free to develop beautiful music. Another important part of Indian music is that it is improvised, and this improvisation arises from the *sruti*, not from the effort of the players but from the gift of revelation from the divine. Perhaps a Western understanding of this process could be that the player is locating and opening himself or herself to grace or the Holy Spirit and is inspired and transformed by this.

In personal formation courses the term 'accompanying' is used to describe an empathic conversation where one person supports another and enables them to explore the full range of emotions, thoughts and consequences of part of their life. Both the accompanied and the accompanist have to listen to each other and are learning and growing from the conversation. However, the accompanist is giving the gift of a platform or space to the accompanied, who is then able to analyse, accept and make plans concerning their current situation. This is an activity which enables great personal growth if those involved are giving high-quality attention, concentration and deep concern. It is an activity which costs. The cost can be in time, energy or space, or in encroaching on personal boundaries. Although it can be measured in these terms it is at a deeper personal level where this cost is felt and there is often an emotional cost to the relationship. One of the saddest stories in the New Testament is where Jesus was with his disciples in Gethsemane: 'He said to them, 'The sorrow in my heart is so great that it almost crushes me. Stay here and keep watch with me' . . . Then he returned to the three disciples and found them asleep' (Matthew 26.38-40). The cost of being there in terms of time was not the issue: it was the emotional and spiritual cost which was too great for the disciples.

The story of Ruth from the Old Testament shows a deep and costly relationship between Ruth and her mother-in-law, Naomi. On Ruth's husband's death she refuses to go back to her family but accompanies Naomi to her home. The quality and cost of the relationship for both women is extraordinary as they work against the odds to become socially integrated and part of the community. In this relationship there is trust, understanding and deep integrity, and the cost to Ruth of this faithful accompanying is apparent.

Although the same ingredients are found in friendship, accompanying is defined by the quality of contact, and in the same way as musicians are often exhausted (and exhilarated) after playing a piece together, there is a similar energy cost in the act of accompanying.

> Penny phoned me on Thursday night just as I'd got in from work. I knew she wanted to talk but I also wondered whether I had enough energy. I asked her to come round in an hour, which gave me enough time to catch my breath and gather my thoughts before she arrived.

We can also use the example of accompanying in athletics. The middle-distance runner may be attempting to beat their personal best time, or to set a new record. In this case a pacemaker will run the first few laps at a faster pace to accompany and encourage, and when their job is done they will break away and leave the athlete to complete their task. In the same way the accompanist may also help set the pace and enable the young person to be stretched as they pursue an idea or thought. As the young person leaves they are 'on their own' in the same way as the athlete completes the race alone, but has been able to draw on the energy and commitment of the accompanist to enable them to address their task or future.

Finally, there is also the picture of someone accompanying us as we are walking along. The road to Emmaus (Luke 24.13-35) is a beautiful story, where the resurrected Jesus walks alongside two followers as they discuss his crucifixion and the events surrounding it. Jesus exerts no pressure on the followers to explain, but gently and sensitively gives them the opportunity to talk about the past few days. The breaking of bread at the end of the conversation in those times was a 'normal' process, rather like offering a cup of tea or coffee to a guest in England. This act was simple and straightforward and, in the light of the circumstances, very profound. In this ordinary process and through his wisdom, the followers suddenly find a sense of peace, and answers to their frantic disturbance. Nothing has changed in one sense, but everything has changed in another.

> It all started with the Junior Choir. Some of them wanted to know more about what they were doing in church and why they were doing it, so about six years ago a group of about half a dozen young people aged between 9 and 15 began meeting at my house after school on Tuesday afternoons.
>
> And what do we do? Well to put it simply we have Bible-based activities which teach about faith and what it means to be a Christian . . .
>
> The other thing that we do is to share a meal together. A proper meal that is; jacket potatoes, shepherd's pie, spaghetti bolognese, that sort of thing, and always with cakes and buns for pudding. Communal eating really binds the group together and more than a few young people over the years have commented that the same effect should be felt by the Church in the Eucharist.
>
> (*Youth A Part*, 1996, p. 80)

Accompanying is a word that has been coined for a very ordinary process, one that occurs in every church and throughout society every day. In one way it is ordinary, in that it is part and parcel of getting on with other people, but it is the quality of accompanying which differentiates it and makes it into a special act which is precious to the person being accompanied. Accompanying happens when one person reaches out and offers himself or herself to another; this may be as a result of a crisis, such as a death or loss, or it may be when someone shares a triumph or achievement. Accompanying also can happen in a faithful way, over a long period, where good support, time and care act as a bedrock for someone who is growing or experiencing long-term difficulties or change. The difference between accompanying and ordinary day-to-day relationships is the quality of the encounter and the cost for the accompanist and the accompanied. The quality of the relationship and the degree of careful attention in listening and supporting require energy and commitment, especially from the accompanist.

Some people are naturally sensitive and aware and are able to perceive the need for accompanying and bring to it the quality that transforms all of their relationships and encounters.

## What accompanying is not

**Accompanying is not counselling.** Although there may be similarities, the purpose of accompanying is not 'analysis' or reflection. There is no 'school' or 'discipline' that is being used within the accompanying relationship. Although there are examples of accompanying there are no formal models or set procedures that an accompanist uses. The aim of counselling is to help a person to analyse and formulate strategies to help them live a fuller life in the future. The aim of accompanying is simply to be close and present at a very human level to the accompanied. There may be similar outcomes from both the counselling and the accompanying relationship, but the method is different. In bereavement, counselling comes only after accompanying has created the environment of support and safety.

**Accompanying is not necessarily befriending.** Befriending has many similar attributes in that the befriender gives non-critical human contact to the person befriended. Also accompanying, like befriending, requires a willingness to engage with the accompanied with an understanding of the privilege of closeness. The essential difference between the two is that befriending usually happens when the person befriended is in distress or has a specific need or crisis. Accompanying can take place for personal and community growth.

**Accompanying is not mentoring.** Although accompanying can happen in a mentoring situation, the mentoring model has an explicit and implicit power dynamic. There is an expectation that the mentor has something that is to be imparted to the mentee. Mentoring comes from the academic field where the mentor imparts knowledge to the pupil. Although there are many mentoring schemes where the relationship is more of an accompanying one, there is a strong sense of imparting knowledge, skills and values from a greater vessel to a lesser one. The notion of accompanying rejects the deficit model of education. The person that is accompanied is seen as a complete person who contains as many answers to their condition as they do questions. Explicit in the process of accompanying is the idea that the best solutions and thoughts are not provided by an expert but are arrived at by the individual himself or herself. The accompanist provides the space and the opportunity to do this.

> One of the hardest things for me is to sit back and see young people 'waste' themselves – getting drunk, taking drugs, smoking, or being in abusive or exploitative relationships. But I know that you don't get anywhere at all by condemning what they are doing. All you can do is to be there and sometimes, when it is going right, the young people draw from your 'being there' to slowly change for the better.

## Ingredients of accompanying

Accompanying is essentially an attitude and a skill which is rooted in the humanity of the accompanist, where the chief quality is the ability to 'be' alongside the accompanied. Although everyone can improve their skill in accompanying there are some people who are exceptionally gifted and we need to identify these people and alert our churches and institutions so that their gifts can be used for the health of all. For a Christian, accompanying can be seen as a reflection of God's nature, and is compassionate, loving and grounded in the concept of free will.

There are some central qualities found in accompanists which are described below:

### Qualities of accompanying

● *Empathy* – ability to tune into the feelings of the accompanied.

● *Sympathy* – not in the sentimental sense but the ability to work in harmony.

● *Tolerance* – ability to be open to a different framework or set of values than are held by the accompanied.

● *Respect for viewpoint of accompanied* – ability to accept that the position of the accompanied has a value not least because it is being held by them.

● *Being grounded or being centred* – ability to act as a stable point around which the accompanied can work. It is therefore essential that he or she is centred, or grounded, and stable enough not to be rocked or troubled by what the accompanied presents. Some accompanists will have found this stability through experience and by reflectively being able to understand and accept themselves. Others will be able to use their faith or beliefs to ground themselves in a framework of stability and reason.

● *Personal space* – having enough personal space available for the process of accompanying. If the accompanist is involved in recovering from something perhaps like the death of a loved one, or a traumatic change in circumstances, they will find it impossible to release enough concentration to work effectively with the accompanied. They will also find that the relationship 'space', which they make for the accompanied, will be invaded by their own grief or problems from their own personal life.

● *Life experience* – ability to use their own life experience as a backdrop to accompanying. This will not intrude on the space of the accompanied but will enrich the understanding of the accompanist.

---

- *Understanding* – ability to understand the young person.

- *Wisdom* – the gift to use life experience and understanding to know when to speak and when to be silent and to discern the profoundly important elements presented in the whole of what the accompanied brings.

- *Active listening* – ability to listen actively and closely and to really hear what is being said.

- *Concentration* – ability to concentrate and be attentive to the whole person whilst accompanying, not just the spoken word.

- *Grace* – ability to be aware of the spirit moving in the time that the accompanist is with the accompanied, and moving on in both their lives afterwards.

## Accompanying young people

Accompanying is especially useful for people when they are trying to think things through, reorder or prioritize their lives. Young people have to do this all the time as they come to terms with their changing physical shape and the changes in their biochemistry and emotions. They also have to manage the changes in their role within the family, choices about relationships, choices about career, choices about style, music, and identity. There is a constant assessment of values and ideas that are important and of how the young person relates to them: should he or she campaign against torture, become vegetarian, go on an anti-road march? There is also the whole unfurling of the 'big' existentialist questions: 'Why am I here?', 'Who am I?', 'Is there a God?' It is at this time that the gift of a wise accompanist is invaluable: not someone who will give answers, but someone who will 'play' an aware background theme which will allow the young person to discover their uniqueness, develop a sense of meaning, and understand their personal vocation.

It is especially important for young people to be given the opportunity to explore their spirituality and to work on the deeper meanings in life. This opportunity for young people is extraordinarily rare at the end of the twentieth century. There is a Christian tradition of spiritual direction, which in many instances is an accompanying relationship that is available to adults. However, there is a distinct reticence in acknowledging that young people and children are spiritual people. A model which is used is that of comparing spiritual growth to the growth of an oak tree. In the same way that an oak tree is a tree and complete whether it is a year old or a hundred years old there is a spiritual existence and completeness whatever the age of the person. Over time the tree will develop layers which are testimony to the times it has passed through – in the same way the older person has laid down experience and understanding on which to draw. The key point is that at any one time there is a sense of completeness and the justification lies in what *is* rather than what will become. Using this we can see that young people have a spiritual existence and should not be viewed only in terms of a spiritual potential.

The accompanist can help the young people not just by offering the space to explore their spirituality and meaning but by giving a chance for the young person to integrate this aspect of their life with the choices and changes that they have to make. Questions like 'What GCSEs do I take?' or 'Shall I live with my girlfriend?' can be explored with reference to the spirituality of the young person and their deeper understanding of themselves and their personal vocation.

## Holistic nature of accompanying

Accompanying is based on the concept of free will. The young person holds and dictates the agenda of the accompanying relationship. The accompanist is invited, by consent of the young person, into the life of the young person. The accompanist provides a framework and structure that enables the young person to explore their agenda. Although different things are discussed it is important that the accompanist is listening to the 'whole' young person. Young people do get opportunities to discuss particular aspects of their lives, for example, what subjects to take, where to go to college, what the latest thing is to listen to or wear. What they do not have is a chance to view themselves as unique beings and to become aware and alert about the personal and individual contribution they can make in their lives. The accompanist can retain an understanding of personal vocation and this provides a central theme which allows young people to see how their own spirituality and sense of meaning infuse all the other decisions that they have to make. Although the subject talked about may well be just one part of the young person's life the accompanist can 'hold' the wider sense of meaning and importance.

## Method of accompanying

Up until now we have talked about accompanying in the abstract, more at the level of values and theoretical parameters than how it is accomplished. This section looks at the method which enables accompanying. One problem we have in setting out a method is that the range of situations where accompanying occurs is extraordinarily varied. It is not like learning to drive a car, where manoeuvres can be explained, demonstrated and copied. It is not a skill which can be taught, although one can become more skilful at accompanying. The main reason for this is that the energy, compassion and attention that the accompanist uses arise from the centre of their being, which for the Christian accompanist is in communion with God. In spite of, or maybe because of, this profound source, the starting point is not the skills of accompanying but creating a 'soft heart' which is receptive and open to grace. This openness and willingness to listen is what provides the space for the young person to explore all aspects of their life, both the peripheral and the deep.

### Time

It is important that there is sufficient time for accompanying. This does not mean that there has to be a dedicated half-hour session; it is more about the attitude of the accompanist, so that the young person thinks 'this person has time for me'. Sometimes this may mean making yourself available, and many instances of accompanying start from the point where the adult has been 'hanging around and wasting time' in the company of young people. Adults send out many 'I am busy' messages to young people, and we live in a society where time is viewed as a commodity which has to be carefully apportioned. The act of accompanying, unlike counselling, happens when the importance is focused on the young person, and there is a realization that the accompanying conversation is something that matters profoundly. Of course both the accompanist and the young person will have other commitments and this has to be understood, but this will be discussed in a straightforward way, and the time element should be seen as a fact to work with, rather than a limiting and defining factor.

## Place

In order for the young person to be able to talk freely, they have to feel comfortable. Therefore it is important to try and choose a place where there will not be interruptions and the conversation cannot be overheard. At the same time it is also important that the young person is not compromised by being in a one-to-one situation alone with the accompanist. The accompanist is also potentially vulnerable in such a situation. There are many suitable places where accompanying can happen quite easily, for example in a coffee bar, after church as people are clearing away, or in a room that is not enclosed with other people about. It can also take place in a house where there are others around in different rooms. It is very important that the good practice of the Children Act 1989 be followed and that the welfare and safety of accompanied young people should be paramount (see also the House of Bishops' statement on child protection, *Protecting All God's Children*, 2004). It is also possible to accompany a group of young people; in this case it is much easier for the Children Act 1989 to be followed, but there are still issues which would have to be talked about and agreed in the group, such as confidentiality.

## Confidentiality

'Confidence' comes from the Latin *con* meaning 'with' and *fides* meaning 'faith'. It is important that the accompanying relationship is 'with faith' and that all confidences are respected. Listening to a young person about things that really matter to them is a great privilege and one that must not be abused. It is important that there is an awareness about confidentiality and that there is a shared understanding, with openness and integrity about how to accompany in confidence or 'with faith'.

How this is worked out in the accompanying relationship is central to the relationship as the accompanist has a mid-path to travel between the confessional of the priest and the prescribed professional practice of the social worker. All accompanists will find themselves at different points on the continuum: what matters is that 'confidence' is observed and that the relationship is one with faith.

It is important that the accompanist should be aware that at times they may feel a need to offload a particularly worrying or difficult time with a young person. At times like these it is important that this happens with integrity and openness. It is not acceptable for the accompanist to chat about the young person they are accompanying and not to respect the integrity of this relationship. Some accompanists will have a friend or colleague that they may talk to so that they can help the young person more effectively , but it is important that if this happens the young person is happy with it.

The relationship of the accompanist and the young person is a special one, so if a discussion takes place it is within the framework of respecting the rights of the young person and respecting the nature of the accompanying. Generally speaking, the content of the session is not discussed in any detail but it may be useful should the accompanist feel anxious, or preoccupied by an accompanying session, for there to be someone available who can share these thoughts and support the accompanist.

The important element in all of this is that the young person should be empowered through the experience of accompanying and that no situation should arise where the accompanist is centre stage and dictating proceedings. The agenda belongs to the young person, not the accompanist, and the young person should always feel confident and in control.

### Relationship
Hearing about deep or close moments in another person's life is an intimate experience and one which is more normally shared amongst close friends. It is important that the accompanist has someone to whom they can talk about the accompanying, so that if there are problems of attraction or fondness these can be addressed. If the experience is rooted in a wider community and there is an awareness of this process of increasing closeness with increasing disclosure, then the accompanist can 'keep the boundaries' and ensure that the relationship continues at a safe level.

### Starting an accompanying relationship

Accompanying does not happen in a time and place separate from everyday life, but is part of everyday living at its best. To 'start' accompanying it is useful to examine the community you live in now and to identify times when you think that existing relationships with young people could be extended and deepened into accompanying. For example, if your church or community runs a youth club it would be reasonably straightforward for there to be people available during the course of the evening for the young people to meet with. This could be introduced informally through one-to-one contact, or could be broached formally to the group:

> We realize that your lives are very busy and there is not the chance to reflect and think through some of the decisions and choices you have to make. There are a few people here who are very happy to listen to anything you think it might be helpful to chat through – where you're going when you leave school, if there is a problem that's troubling you, what you might want to do in the rest of your life. Anything you say will be confidential. The reason for our doing this is that we realize that in our own pasts there have been people who have given us time, and this has really helped us. As life is so busy now there are fewer people with time to spare so we are happy to give you this time if you'd like to talk through anything.

This could also be offered through visits to schools, work with the uniformed organizations, or any other contact that you have with young people.

### The first meeting

It is necessary in the first accompanying meeting to make sure that both of you (or the group) are clear about the 'ground rules'. This does not have to be long-winded or legalistic but means that you check out things like time, place, and confidentiality so that both of you are comfortable. It is useful to start with the accompanist saying what they understand by accompanying and explain how the agenda, pace and depth of conversation is set by the young person and not by them.

Taking time to agree the 'ground rules' means that:

- You are both comfortable about the amount of time you have available, and the place where you are talking.

- You are showing the young person that you are treating them as an adult. This demonstrates that you respect them and feel they have as much right as you to negotiate the basics of the accompanying relationship.

- By explaining that the agenda, pace and depth of the accompanying are set by the young person, you are showing them that they are in control in the relationship.

If you are working with a group of young people the same issues need to be agreed, along with additional elements such as the need for respect concerning anything said in the group, and a process being agreed to ensure that everyone has a chance to speak.

### Choosing an accompanist

The accompanist makes the decision to be available; the young person makes the choice as to whether they are going to work with them. Everyone makes decisions about who they are comfortable with, and the process by which someone asks you to be their accompanist is similar to the musical situation. Professional musicians choose who they want to work with, and their choice may not necessarily be the 'best' pianist, but the pianist whose style or approach is close to their own. They will be looking for an accompanist who will bring out their own particular style of playing and enable them to explore their individual gift. Choosing an accompanist is more of a matching process than a 'better or worse' process. However, the prospective accompanist has to be confident within themselves of managing the situation when a young person chooses not to work with them. If the prospective accompanist perceives this as a rejection then this is an indication that they themselves have a need to be wanted and they may not have the space to offer to the young person anyway. If the offer of the accompanist is not taken up then the accompanist should be prepared to 'drop back' and leave the young person alone. It is important that the accompanist takes this in their stride and does not 'act the martyr'.

The accompanist is not a saint or some sort of super-person. They are simply people who are willing to be available, to be attentive, focused, and to respect the young person with whom they are working. If these qualities are offered openly and with integrity many young people will accept the opportunity and grab it with both hands.

## What is achieved through accompanying

It is important when considering any action to understand why that action has been chosen and what it is hoped will be achieved. It is not enough to do something because it is 'a good thing'. Part of youth work practice involves planning, setting objectives and having some process of evaluation which checks whether these objectives have been met. One of the difficulties in assessing whether accompanying is useful is that the benefit is often felt much later on in life.

> One day an older man came into our centre and handed me an envelope with a cheque. I asked him what this was for and he said that when he was a young teenager people at the centre had helped him out and had time for him. He was just retiring and as part of the farewell there was a collection for charity. He had nominated the youth centre to receive this collection.

This man had recognized the benefit of the work throughout his adult life, but he did not 'feed back' to those who had helped him. In fact by the time he went back to the club those people who 'accompanied' him could well be in their eighties or even have died. Almost everyone has someone in their past who has had time for them and helped them in this way. This illustrates and evidences the long-term benefit of accompanying – which we carry with us throughout our lives.

As a child I was something of a rebel and the way most of my teachers handled this was to 'sit on me' and try and close me down. My teacher, Miss Golding, in the second year juniors realized I had potential and 'believed in me'. She had one of my poems published and I had a real place in the class. Thirty-five years later I was scanning a disk of all the phone numbers in the United Kingdom and thought I would try and locate her. I knew her married name was unusual and when I looked it up there were only six names in the directory. I decided to phone all of these and at the third attempt found her. I was so emotional and tears were streaming down my face when I told her how much her time and belief in me had mattered and affected me. Through the years and even now, I am able to draw on her confidence in me and acceptance of me to help me get through difficult situations and work with vision.

It is also possible to see the short-term effects of accompanying. There are numerous times when a person is so knotted up with indecision or crisis that in effect they cease to function. At these times the accompanist can provide a strong, consistent presence which will give them space to unravel their concerns and enable them to find a sense of order and to think of what they can do next.

In these cases there is often spontaneous feedback: 'Thanks for that, I feel I know what I want to do now', or 'I haven't solved anything but at least I know why I am doing it' are the sorts of responses that may be forthcoming. If the feedback is not spontaneous this can be prompted, not 'fishing for compliments' but asking in an adult way if the process was helpful and if it can be changed in any way.

In accompanying, the young person takes responsibility for their life and has the major input into the nature of the sessions by bringing the agenda, setting the pace and deciding at what depth to discuss things. When such an adult relationship has been established it is easy to ask frankly about the usefulness of the process.

## Peer accompanying

In most of the examples above there has been the expectation that the accompanist is an older person and the accompanied a young person. This is not necessarily the case, and in fact there is no reason why it could not be the other way round with the accompanist younger than the accompanied.

The most likely alternative to an older accompanist and younger accompanied is when the accompanist is a similar age to the accompanied; this is called peer accompanying. There are advantages to being similar in age, in that there is an understanding between the accompanist and the young person of the culture, relationships and life factors. The rapport can be established quickly, and the young person can identify readily with an accompanist who is their own age. One of the few disadvantages in peer accompanying is that the accompanist will be dealing with their own teenage transition and may not have sufficient personal space to offer time and attention to someone else's life. An older accompanist will also be drawing on a larger bank of experiences and may be able to give a longer-term perspective than a young accompanist.

## Conclusion

Accompanying is a difficult term to pin down and define. We have all experienced it in some form at some time in our lives and have enjoyed great benefits from the attention and respect of others. The fact that it is difficult to define does not stop us from being able to recognize it. Once we identify accompanying and appreciate it we can make a decision to enrich and expand its use, both personally and in the groups to which we belong.

Although the term is vague there are elements of 'good practice' which are essential to accompanying. The young person must always be safe, physically and mentally, and be given every opportunity to negotiate and agree the process. Similarly, the elements of 'good practice' will safeguard the accompanist, both physically and emotionally, and these should be in place at the start of the accompanying relationship. These elements of good practice are addressed first of all and then will become part of the background as the young person works with the accompanist.

The accompanist is offering an opportunity that is unique and life-enhancing for the young person involved. This is the stuff of the Gospels, the heart of Christianity, to be there for each other, and is a precious gift that the adults of the Church can give to younger members.

# 4

# Examples of accompanying

## Introduction

Accompanying describes the quality of the relationship. It does not focus on doing but being. This chapter brings together a collection of relationships where the quality of accompanying is present. The situations are very different but that profound quality of accompanying is apparent. In the first example a young woman is supported by her youth group but it is the youth worker who takes this further by accompanying her.

> Chris is a 13-year-old who is very fashionable, dresses much older than her years and would pass easily for a 16-year-old. Within the church youth group she has no close friends of her own age. She is very full of her own opinions and at her school hangs out with a particular gang who definitely do not go to church. She comes from a Christian family, but they are fairly relaxed about whom she has as friends. We give her the space and time to have her say. A youth worker from our group regularly takes her out for a burger meal, away from parents, youth group or school friends, and gives her space to be heard and listened to in an environment where she feels comfortable.

Accompanying is a natural process. The accompanist starts from where the young person is – their enthusiasms, their interests or their problems. In the following example the accompanist started the relationship by building on an interest in outdoor activities.

Mark loved outdoor activity, but was very low on confidence. At 16 years he was out of work and limited in both finance and opportunity.

As an older member of the youth group he was asked to work together with the youth worker to design and run some outside games for a weekend event. As a result he discovered new abilities in organization and leadership. After three or four such events the funding was found through a local charity and the Parish Council to send Mark on an outdoor leadership course. The youth worker had almost to cajole Mark to take part and in the end he only went on condition that the youth worker went as well.

Over the ensuing years, six in all, Mark's brother and mother died, his girlfriend became pregnant and had an abortion, Mark was married to another young woman but the marriage lasted only six months. Throughout this time, the youth worker was around for Mark and, on occasion, initiated discussion on where things were at. The youth worker's understanding was that his role was to enable and support Mark in these traumatic experiences, occasionally offering options and opportunities for Mark himself to work with or act in relation to issues faced, but on the whole working at 'being there' alongside Mark at times of crisis.

This simple starting point, of building on an interest in outdoor activity, along with the time and energy that the youth worker put into the process, eventually led to Mark's gaining both summer and winter mountain leadership qualifications, becoming a part-time paid youth worker and, in the process, growing in both confidence and self-awareness.

In the last example the accompanist started with Mark's interest and gave him space and support. Not only did Mark's interest and outdoor skills improve but there was considerable personal gain and development. Sometimes young people's agendas differ from our own. They may decide to embark on a course of action which creates problems for themselves. In the following example the young person has a natural desire to change the church and drives towards this aim. Sometimes in situations like this, young people are unaware of the impact they have when 'just saying it as it is' and may be rebutted or face resistance. It takes courage on the part of the accompanist to be alongside young people as they break new ground, and challenge church structures.

> Tony has led a very sheltered life in a rural community, brought up by his grandparents, extremely shy when it came to meeting the opposite sex, etc. . . . He became involved in local church activities and then got involved in regional youth work. He tended to take on many responsibilities which he could not cope with. I befriended him over a number of years as he later became a member of our National Youth Committee. I was able to share my own life experiences, usually over the telephone, since meetings were difficult because the distance was great and support was not easily available in the local context. I offered advice and suggestions and managed to encourage him to prioritize his voluntary time. I was there at the end of the telephone for him. He actually stood for a major youth post as his confidence was built up; he has purchased his own flat, got stable employment and also now does voluntary work as an agent for a political party (not one of my choosing!). He is a good example of long-distance accompanying.

If a young person has had a good experience of church or a particular project they may be open to new experience and opportunities. Having an accompanist, or someone they can trust to speak with, can help them to discern which opportunities are right for them and which may prove difficult. In the following example Ben was able to use his contacts at church to check out a decision he had made when he was approached by a couple at the local bookshop.

One day Ben was on our doorstep at 5 p.m., our afternoon teatime. He was confused and slightly stressed. In the town he had visited the local bookshop to purchase a Bible, because he had not got one at home. He had browsed in the religious section, then ordered the Bible he wanted, and on leaving was approached by a young couple, who asked him what he had ordered. Taken aback by this he began to tell them. They were a nice, well-spoken, well-dressed young couple. They stated that they were Christians and advised a particular Bible, invited him round for coffee, and asked for his telephone number. He did not give his number, but took their calling card. They were from the International Church of Christ, a well-known cult that particularly specializes in targeting young Christians. We were able to assure Ben that he did the sensible thing and tried to explain what ICC was all about. To Ben as a new Christian it took some explaining because on the surface this couple seemed very sincere and genuine. He was able to knock on our door straight after college and we were able to help; because we had built up a trustful relationship, he came to us straight away. We were able to alert other youth networks in the town to the presence of the cult and take appropriate action.

Accompanying is often a long-term relationship and can provide a significant balance and support for a young person who is carrying a difficult home situation. In the next example this help has been given to Rachel. Central to this relationship is the developing faith of Rachel and this has been at the heart of the accompanying.

I have only known Rachel a little over a year. She came away on pilgrimage to Iona last summer. She has been very involved with her church – bell-ringing, serving and as a lone young person in their worship group. Her parents are very authoritarian and her home life is difficult – parents constantly rowing, her friends not allowed in the house, her activities restricted (including her church activities). Her faith is strong and has helped her a lot, but she wants to talk about it and her life. Our relationship since Iona has been largely through letter-writing (at some length) as she lives at the other end of the county. We have had some phone calls but her parents dislike my ringing her. Both the writing and the receiving of letters seem to help her sort out her priorities and cope with her home life. During the winter she has come close to moving out of her home, and has considered moving up country to join a boyfriend, but the thought of the disruption this would cause to her education helped her decide to stick it out at home. She takes A levels this summer and hopes to go to university.

Supporting Rachel has been very much a two-way thing. She has supported me by helping with in-service training for clergy and with a weekend for younger teenagers.

Some people seem to be natural accompanists and accompany different people over many years. In the next example Dorothy's life has obviously touched many of those in the church, both young and old, and the tribute shown by the teenagers when she died is a testimony to this.

Dorothy was an elderly lady who just liked people. She had lived in the parish much of her life and had seen the church built. In her later years she visited her 'old people', many of them only a couple of years older than herself.

Dorothy always had a smile and unfailingly gave sweets to the young children but they loved her more for the attention she gave them.

As they grew older and graduated to the choir she would always ask how they were getting on at school. She showed an interest in their confirmation preparation and I'm sure that she prayed for them. She made a point of coming to the confirmation services even when they were at other churches in the deanery, and encouraged the young people by her kind words and uncritical smile.

When Dorothy died the teenagers were determined to go to the funeral so that they could sing in the choir for her. Kelly asked to read a prayer she had written in thanksgiving for Dorothy's life and to say goodbye. When it came to the funeral and I stood beside Kelly to read the prayers, Kelly could not read for the tears, and so I read for her. For me, those tears showed the relationship between one elderly woman and the young people 70 years younger than herself whom she had accompanied.

Although in most cases accompanying 'just happens' it can be encouraged in a church or project. In the following example a simple exercise was used in the church service. Following on from this many of the young people carried on talking to 'their' member of the congregation and the older people continued to be interested in the lives of the younger members and continued to pray for them.

One rural parish in Devon, keen to enable young people to develop relationships with older members of the congregation, decided to try out an idea. Each young person was asked to write down two things for which they would value prayer and was then, after the morning service, encouraged to ask an older member of the congregation to take their piece of paper and, during the coming week, to pray for them. Each slip contained the following kind of information:

| | |
|---|---|
| My name is: | Catherine |
| I am: | 13 years old |
| Please pray for: | Request one |
| | Request two |

After the following week's service, the same young people were encouraged to repeat the exercise and give their slips to the same adults. The conversations that ensued even after the first week were very significant, with congregation members asking 'their' young person how things were in relation to what they had prayed for.

From this small beginning a few strong and ongoing bonds were formed and many of the adults took it so seriously that they began to approach 'their' young person to seek out items for prayer.

When asked why they had chosen particular adults the young people responded with comments like:

'She used to be my Sunday School teacher.'

'He looked a nice old man.'

'She helped me when I fell off my bike.'

'He smiles at me every Sunday.'

This process enabled some adults to see their role as accompanists, even if for a short time. Their awareness grew out of growing concern initiated by the young people involved.

If accompanying is recognized and valued it can move from something that happens 'by accident' and incidentally to being something highly prized and encouraged. The following project seems to have the spirit of accompanying as its very backbone. It runs through the work and forms the central ethic of the work.

On the Edge is a piece of Christian youth work based on long-term commitment and a model of accompanying. Steve, the project leader, has been committed to young people in the Tiverton area for nearly twelve years. Each Thursday night he and a small team of volunteers take their double-decker bus to the main car park and run a coffee shop and meeting place for young people in the town. Over the years literally hundreds of young people have used the bus, some for whole evenings, some for minutes; some for a few weeks, some for many months or years. The main purpose of this piece of work has been relationship-building: 'being there' for the young people they encounter; being willing to pick up issues and concerns as young people raise them. In effect it has been looking to act as Jesus did in the Emmaus story through listening to what is uppermost on young people's agenda and occasionally helping them see through the pain and hurt as well as celebrating their joys and achievements. There have been times when the pressure to show results in terms of Christian commitment amongst the young people has been very great, but always resisted. However, the number of young people who use Steve and his team members as a point of reference because they are 'always there' is most significant. Accompanying young people can never be about the accompanist's agenda. It must always give the kind of space and commitment that the On the Edge team provide. In this way the accompanist becomes a vital point of reference, even if only referred to from a distance.

In the following example there was an obvious awareness of the isolation and apprehension of young people as they find themselves arrested and taken into police custody. This need was identified and a solution was to assemble a group of volunteers to be available to accompany young people as they arrive at the cells. This example shows how the spirit of accompanying can be incorporated into a project. It is important to realize, however, that even when a project has been set up in this way the crucial input is given by the volunteer to the young person. For this to be accompanying it has to be working to the young person's agenda and with the spirit of accompanying.

Surrey Appropriate Adult Volunteer Scheme is managed for Guildford Diocesan Council for Social Responsibility by the Reverend Peter Knapper in partnership with the Social Services of Surrey County Council, the Surrey and Metropolitan Police Services and the Safer Surrey Partnership Team.

The scheme deploys 68 trained volunteers to support vulnerable suspects on police custody sites throughout Surrey during 'out of hours' times: that means in the evenings, nights and early mornings of weekdays and at all times of day and night on Saturdays and Sundays. The volunteers come from a wide background of age and experience. Some are in work, others are at home most of the time as retired people or householders. Many have been recruited through church networks and regard their work as part of their Christian service to a neighbour in need. The clients are usually classed as vulnerable by the custody sergeant and therefore in need of support, especially during the police interview that helps decide whether they are to be charged, cautioned or bailed.

At the end of the process the volunteer completes an attendance form that gives basic details about the case so that a picture can be built up of the demand for the service and the way the demand is being met. In particular cases where there is seen to be an urgent social need information is shared with the helping agencies, particularly the Youth Justice Team or Social Services.

Young people and especially boys aged 15 to 16 make up the bulk of those who are seen. The next highest category is male adults with learning disability. Girls and women have a lower offending rate, but their cases can be very distressing, especially if they are pregnant or the mothers of small children.

During a recent weekend Edna from Reigate reported on supporting a 16-year-old boy from Redhill arrested on charges of criminal damage, being drunk and disorderly and escaping from lawful custody. 'He told me he was too drunk to really remember anything.' He was seen at 9.30 a.m. on Saturday morning and later released on bail. That same morning she also supported a 16-year-old boy from Caterham on charge of burglary. In both these cases parents were unwilling to attend. On the previous Thursday evening Roberta from Pirbright supported a 16-year-old boy from a town near Guildford who was living in a tent. He was suspected of stealing from his own family and as victims of his offence they are prevented from acting for him but are also unwilling to act. Roberta advised him to seek help for accommodation and a training place.

Since the scheme began in 1995 in Woking the volunteers have supported over 1,300 vulnerable suspects in Woking, Guildford, Reigate and Staines. They supplement the work of Youth Justice, Social Services and the Emergency Duty team and work in teams so that they are on call once in four or five weeks at a time. They have shown a high degree of commitment to their work and to the young people whom they accompany through the justice process.

Where the ethic of accompanying is deeply rooted in a project all members of staff may be sensitized to this and can be available for young people. In the following example different members of staff in the project have been able to accompany Carl over many years.

> Carl is a 21-year-old very capable young man, who is a member of a youth project and coaches the project's football team. However, his life has had its ups and downs. Six months ago he went through a very difficult period where he was unable to get steady work. Also at this time his girlfriend was pregnant and the relationship eventually broke down.
>
> Carl is an only child and has always been very close to his mother, but was also going through a very stressful time with her. He became very depressed and felt that he did not know where he was going and that his life had lost all direction, and he had contemplated suicide. Carl continued to come to the project during this time, often sitting talking with staff for about half an hour. This was helpful as he found friendship, support and someone who was away from the family. He also found that being able to give something positive to other young people took his mind off his own problems and made him feel better about himself.
>
> Carl has moved on, he found work and has recently had a promotion and he continues to work successfully with young people and to find support from the project.

In the last two examples it can be seen how accompanying can become part of the work of the project. The next example starts from a formal position where the youth worker offers to work alongside the young person. The description of this accompanying story shows just how difficult it can be to accompany another person.

In a previous full-time youth work post I worked with a 19-year-old young woman called Jane who had a 13-month-old daughter, Chloe. Jane and Chloe had been coming to the centre where I worked for several months, but one of my project workers had mainly dealt with Jane prior to my involvement. Jane's daughter Chloe was suddenly taken into care one weekend due to allegations of physical child abuse. Chloe was in the care of Jane and her partner Michael at the time of the allegation. A neighbour of Jane's was looking after Chloe when she became concerned about severe bruising on her body; she called the police, who took the child to the local hospital, and the child was then subsequently taken into care. In the doctors' considered opinion, backed up by photographic evidence, the bruises were clearly caused by an adult hand slapping the child and by punching. Both Jane and Michael (who was not Chloe's father) were arrested and subsequently charged.

My involvement came about as a result of Jane coming into the centre in a very distressed state and asking for our help. I spent several hours talking to Jane, who was adamant that she had not caused Chloe's injuries and initially was adamant that Michael had not caused them either. Jane was suspected of having mild learning difficulties and was very confused and bewildered by all the case conferences and court proceedings that she now faced. I asked her if she wanted me to support her during all of these proceedings, which she did, and I explained very clearly to her my role: that I was there to support her, not to make a judgement on whether she was innocent or guilty, but to help her to understand all of the proceedings and to support her in representing herself to the authorities. Over the next few months I accompanied Jane to case conferences, core group meetings (this is a small group that is set up by the Chair of the case conference and includes parties who have a direct involvement in the child's welfare, e.g. parents, grandparents, foster carers, health visitor and social worker, and meets more frequently to review the situation than the case conferences) and meetings with her solicitor. I also accompanied Jane to court on several occasions and to meetings with her social worker.

My involvement with the authorities in this case was positive: they accepted that Jane needed someone there to support her and they were prepared to accept me in this role once they had checked out my credentials. I believe that if I had been an unqualified youth worker they would not have been as prepared to accept my involvement. My involvement with this case lasted for several months and during that time it became important to remind the different agencies that I was there to support Jane and not to take sides or to monitor her behaviour. I was asked by the solicitor for Social Services to prepare a formal statement for them but I refused to do this as it would have been used as part of a case against Jane, and although my statement would not intentionally have contained anything negative about her relationship with Chloe I did not feel it was appropriate to make one.

My feelings during this case were varied. I found it quite difficult to support Jane when I was not 100 per cent certain about the facts. Abuse had been committed and from both Jane and Michael's statements it was clear that either Jane or Michael had committed the abuse and neither of them denied this, but they would also not accuse each other of the abuse. This was quite frustrating, especially as the authorities clearly believed Michael was responsible and Jane's refusal to implicate Michael was clearly jeopardizing her future with Chloe. My feelings were further complicated when some of the decisions Jane made were clearly not in Chloe's best interests. I also found it very frustrating when Jane made decisions that I felt were wrong, but I had to support her in those decisions.

> I think the two main learning points from this situation for me were: (a) the need to constantly remind the authorities involved of my role and to be clear about that myself, and (b) the need to assure the young person of support whilst not taking sides.

Accompanying can take place in any setting. The following example comes from a parish where there is no established provision for young people as the church believes 'it has no young people'. There is, however, a member of the congregation who carries out an effective ministry with individual young people outside of a formal youth work setting. This is in a parish which is of a traditional Anglo-Catholic orientation and serves a parish of some 16,000 people in an area which was formerly heavily populated by traditional and heavy industries. It now has problems of decay and abandonment associated with closure of this type of industry. There are two examples of accompanying here: both illustrate the cost to the accompanist. The second example shows that accompanying is a risky business and some young people may abuse the trust and the relationship. It is important to note this, not to put people off, but to show that accompanying is a very real relationship, taking place in a very real world, and although through this some people are able to draw strength and move forwards, some young people are not able to do this.

> May, now in her late thirties, moved to the parish a couple of years ago, having lived and worked in different areas of the country. Her particular skills are in counselling and pre-school education and she combines part-time work as a professional counsellor with voluntary work in special education schools. It was through this latter link that she came into contact with Chris, whom she knew to be a young person living in the parish.

Chris, 13 years old, is described by the agencies that intervene in his life as 'a child with behavioural difficulties'. May was initially engaged in helping Chris with his reading development and this made slow progress at first. Over time it became clear that it was simply not possible to develop Chris's reading through the range of material that was being put forward through the school and that the written word contained only frustration and anger for him. The combination of academic frustration and family difficulties often meant that Chris's responses to the world were withdrawal or violence. May realized it was only by grasping Chris's attention through physically involving him in things that he could feel interested in reading about it. Church provided a very good option for him to experience something that he could then go on to read about. May began to take Chris to church with her, after negotiation with his parents, and there he rapidly became engrossed in the structure of the services and the building and began to read books based on Bible stories. He is now going through confirmation classes and has been trained as a server in the church. His reading has developed enormously and he consumes books at a rate that the education system would not have thought possible for him. May has encouraged him to think highly of himself and to respect others in the way that he deals with them. The violence and withdrawal have almost completely stopped now and this has eased the pressure on the family as a whole, although this is not the end of their difficulties.

The second young person that May was to work with individually was Chris's sister Amanda. Amanda is approaching 16 and whereas the majority of her contemporaries are working towards qualifications, Amanda has decided that school is 'a crock of shit', and she wants nothing to do with it. Her parents agonize over her skipping school and the hours spent in the company of the wrong sort of kids in shopping malls, smoking, drinking and thieving. Her mother is extremely patient and forgiving, but her father does not know what to do about Amanda. Issues came to a head several weeks before Christmas when, after her father uncovered some lies that Amanda had told to him, he packed a bag for her and threw her out. May had been meeting with Amanda for several weeks now to discuss the issue of lying and to help her deal better with the situations in her life when she felt that this was necessary. May had believed that things were going well. She could not bear to see Amanda homeless and took her into her own house at this point. In dealing with this May also sought the advice of her Diocesan Youth Advisor, who made approaches to several organizations for assistance and was eventually able to find a place in a Christian-run hostel for her, although it would not be available for several weeks.

May continued to allow Amanda to stay with her but the relationship deteriorated as Amanda continued to spin an ever more complex web of deceits, which developed into her stealing from May and attempting to disrupt the lives of the people around May who were trying to help and be supportive. May continued to be a visitor and supporter when Amanda moved into the hostel, but it quickly became clear that Amanda was playing exactly the same games with the workers and other residents there.

Amanda eventually told hostel workers that an uncle was ill and she had to go and visit for a few days, and she has not returned. May similarly has had no further contact with her but is aware through her continuing relationship with Chris that she has visited the family home occasionally. May continues to pray for Amanda and receives support from her network of friends.

In all of these examples the accompanied person is young and we have argued that it is a valuable resource for young people. However, accompanying is a resource for people of all ages and as a postscript the next example is one where an older person has been accompanied.

Mary was a regular member of the congregation at church and I also enjoyed going round to see her for coffee some mornings. Although elderly, she was very young at heart and enjoyed a good laugh. One day she phoned me sounding really sad, saying she did not want to tell me something that would upset me. Still only thinking of others, she had to tell me the news that she had cancer of the liver and had only a short time to live.

During the few weeks that we had left I visited Mary regularly and as she was finding it increasingly difficult to read I started reading to her, the latest Catherine Cookson book, a chapter every time I went to see her. As time grew short, Mary was getting very tired, and sometimes when I called she just said 'Hello' and held my hand but could not listen to the story. Still, we were determined to finish the book so we had the idea of putting it on a tape, then whenever Mary wanted to listen to it she could. People said she could get tapes from the library, but Mary said they would not be like her tapes. These always had a personal message at the end, just for her.

Mary was taken into the hospice where she had one week before she died. On my last visit to her there she told me she had finished the book. The next day she died peacefully.

# 5

# Further thoughts on developing accompanying

## Introduction
By now, you will have a good idea about what we mean by accompanying. All of the examples in the last chapter will bring to mind a huge number of occasions when accompanying has happened and there have been positive results for the young people concerned. Although you have many pictures and probably an understanding of what accompanying is, it will probably be difficult for you to try to define accompanying. This is because accompanying is a quality, an essential state of being which lies deep in all of the examples described before. You may not be able to define accompanying but you may well be able to *know* accompanying and be able to identify it when you see it.

In training sessions within the Church you may have been asked to think of those people who have been significant to you in the past. Those people who have given you time, wisdom, or have 'been there' when you needed them. When asked, we do not look for a definition of 'significant' because it strikes a chord in our own experience and we move on to the task of reflecting on those people who have been there for us.

In order for your own accompanying to develop it is important that you are able to identify it. We hope that this chapter will help you to identify accompanying, be alert to it and work with it to develop your own skills and gift of being an accompanist for others. Also you may wish to seek an accompanist for yourself when it would benefit you.

## Accompanying in the past
A useful exercise is to reflect on your past life and identify all of those who have accompanied you. Some of these people will have been

significant to you over a long period of time; others will have had an impact on your life even though your contact with them may have been very brief. What was significant about these people? What did you value about the contact? Was there anything within the relationship that was not helpful? How did these relationships change your life?

Another exercise is to think back into the past over the times when you have accompanied others. It is sometimes very difficult to acknowledge that we may have enabled someone else to change their life, or that we may have given something significant to someone else just by 'being there'. Allow yourself to realize how your accompanying may have helped other people. Think back to specific occasions. What made the encounter special? Was there anything you would want to change in the relationship? How did you benefit from being an accompanist?

It will be helpful if you are able to discuss these experiences with a colleague, as they may be able to extend your recollection and help you to understand where you already have been accompanying and the tremendous worth of the process.

## Accompanying in the present

As well as locating accompanying incidents in the past there are almost certainly experiences of accompanying which are happening now. Take some time to think through your own life and identify the people to whom you would turn if you had a crisis now. Who would be able to give you space and time to reflect and accompany you?

Also think about those who are turning to you at the moment, or would be in contact should they need to talk things through, or rejoice about an achievement. Think about odd occasions when you have been able to reach out to someone in openness and without prescribing the outcome. If you are having difficulty with this exercise, don't worry, it is sometimes difficult, especially for Christians, to acknowledge that they have been able to meet others at a profound level.

Again, if you are able to discuss this with a colleague you may be able to prompt each other and discuss what accompanying relationships you are involved with at the moment.

## Accompanying in our church or organization

The accompanist is not alone, but invariably part of a range of groups, or networks. If a church or a group feels that accompanying is important it will make time to identify this and enable it to happen and develop. If you consider your own church or organization you can reflect on who are the 'natural' accompanists in the group. When Paul called Barnabas 'the one who encourages' (Acts 4.36) it was because he had identified in Barnabas the quality of being alongside others and encouraging them. In any group and especially within our churches there are people who spend a lot of time being available for others. These are not the directive sorts who insist on giving advice or running other people's lives, but those who will 'be there' when they are needed.

It was several years before I found out that one woman in our congregation tirelessly supported the minister. It was not obvious, but Joyce was extremely perceptive and would give quality attention to how the minister was feeling. Sometimes, she would send a card, or deliver a cake to the Manse, if things were particularly rough. Other times she would gently but firmly point out if he had been insensitive or unthinking. Joyce was not, like many 'helpers', fussy or obvious, but took her self-chosen task seriously, which enabled the minister to extend his work and feel good about himself.

Joyce was a 'natural' and would think it strange that this was anything out of the ordinary, or that it was something that should be noted and praised. However, it is important that this act of accompanying should be noted and affirmed. Paul did identify Barnabas' gift by calling him an encourager. This was not to inflate Barnabas' ego but to acknowledge the time, energy and effort that Barnabas had spent on building up others, and Paul is saying that this is good.

It is because in the West we see things from the perspective of individual ego that we are concerned that praise will 'go to people's heads' and they will become unbearable. Acknowledgement and affirmation can be part of the culture of an organization, without its being ego-based. The aim is not to build up a cult of encouraging or heighten accompanying above other aspects of the church or organization's work. Rather it is to acknowledge and accept this as a precious and important element in the group. Paul does give a warning on how gifts of the Spirit can be highjacked to feed personal egos in 1 Corinthians 14. His vision of how gifts can be used well is illustrated in 1 Corinthians 12 where he uses the model of the inter-dependent body.

Our concern is that accompanying is not seen as a vital organ or part of the body of work of the Church, and when there is pressure on the organization then accompanying can get squeezed out by more functional tasks.

There is, however, a problem about labelling and identifying accompanying. Accompanying is not a task, a skill or a capacity, it arises out of the sense of being. Although there is often behaviour related to accompanying, the behaviour is an indication of what is happening, not the accompanying itself.

Let us go back to the symbol 'to listen' which was explained in the Introduction. The elements which make up the character also identify key areas in listening: the ear to hear, the eye to see, the heart for a quality rooted in the emotions, you, the key person involved and undivided attention. Some of these are observable, you can see whether a person is looking at you, you can tell if they have heard you, and you can also detect how much of their attention they are giving you. Some of these are more difficult to detect – how much are they listening with their heart, and how much are they thinking of you or 'you in theory' or 'themselves as you'. It is a question of tuning yourself to observe and reflect on where accompanying happens in your own group, and looking intuitively at the way people relate to each other.

After a while it becomes easier to identify accompanying and then you can take steps to help encourage it. We have already mentioned the difficulty in praising people with particular skills or gifts. This is only a problem if the desire to be rewarded and to be seen to be doing something special over-rides and masks the rewards of the act of accompanying itself. If we are alert to the possibility of an 'accompanying elite' forming we can take steps to ensure that this does not happen. What does need to happen is for the acts of accompanying to be observed and affirmed.

Churches and other organizations have become very 'busy' in the last twenty years or so. There is increasing activity in churches as groups for toddlers, women, men, the elderly, the unemployed are formed and run by members of the congregation. There are also the financial pressures on organizations to diversify in order to maintain buildings and the work. It is because accompanying is not 'an activity' that it can get overlooked in the functional tasks within an organization. One way of ensuring that this does not happen is if it is located at the heart of the organization and time and resources are set aside to enable accompanying. Accompanying should be seen as a central role of the Church. It is interesting to note that when people reflect on their faith journey it is not preaching or worship which is given primary significance, but an individual or group which has given them time. This central role is achieved when the group realizes the importance of relationships and the effect of giving undivided attention, and enables the space for this to happen within their church or organization.

It is important when accompanying is valued within the church or organization that it should remain grounded and retain integrity, and that the life-giving nature of accompanying should not be regimented by definition and prescription. While it is perfectly in order to challenge one another and reflect on accompanying practice, it is important to realize that the power to be an accompanist comes from a person's deepest integrity, which for the Christian is rooted in God.

## Ensuring good practice in accompanying

There are two classic organizational reactions to dealing with intuitive and creative actions such as accompanying. The first is to control them and to define them into channels that the organization is able to manage. The second is to leave the creative person in a mystical aura and not dare to interfere with the 'wonderful gift'. The danger of the first is that the creativity and heart of the work are squeezed from it and what is left is a functional, defined shell. The danger of the second is that creative and intuitive people are not grounded in a system of support and accountability and are vulnerable to 'going off the rails'.

It is possible to have a system of support and accountability which enables the work to be rooted in personal integrity and power, within the wider framework of the organization or church. Thus an accompanist should feel that there is someone, or a group, that they could go to within the organization if there are problems or difficulties arising from the relationship that they have with the young person. The organization must retain the ability to challenge the practice of the accompanist to ensure that the young people who are being accompanied are not disadvantaged or vulnerable. It is therefore very important that accompanying a young person is in accordance with the Children Act 1989 and all other elements of good practice are in place. Our experience is that when people view this creatively they come up with a range of solutions which enable accompanying to happen in all sorts of ways.

## And now?

If you have felt encouraged or inspired by the idea of accompanying and by the examples in this book you may be wondering what you do next. There is good news and bad news: the bad news is that there is no prescribed route for developing accompanying and the good news is that there is no prescribed route for developing accompanying.

Accompanying is something you come to know about from experience. A book like this may help open your eyes and give you words to describe something that you have known all of your life and something which you would like to develop.

As authors of this book we are not intending to write a definitive work, one which dots all of the i's and crosses all the t's. Rather we see the act of writing and the act of reading as part of the accompanying. Our hope is that the book will start a dialogue, giving accompanying a name so that we can talk about it, work with it and come to know it and ourselves better.

# Bibliography

Sarah Banks (ed.), *Ethical Issues in Youth Work*, Routledge, 1999.

William Bloom (ed.), *The New Age*, Rider, 1991.

David R. Blumenthal, *God at the Centre – Meditations on Jewish Spirituality*, Jason Aronson, 1994.

Board of Education of the General Synod, *Youth A Part*, National Society/Church House Publishing, 1996.

John Bowlby, *Child Care and the Growth of Love*, Penguin, 1953.

T.S. Eliot, *The Complete Poems and Plays*, Faber & Faber, 1969.

Paulo Freire, *Pedagogy of the Oppressed*, Penguin, 1995.

Paulo Freire, *Pedagogy of Hope: Reliving Pedagogy of the Oppressed*, Penguin, 1996.

Roy M. Gasnick OFM, *The Francis Book – 800 Years with the Saint from Assisi*, Collier, 1980.

Kahlil Gibran, *Jesus – The Son of Man. His Words and his Deeds*, Oneworld, 1993.

Good News Bible, The Bible Societies, 1976.

David Ray Griffin (ed.), *Sacred Interconnections – Postmodern Spirituality, Political Economy, and Art*, State University of New York, 1990.

HMI report, 'Effective youth work', *Education Observed*, 6, HMSO, 1987, pp. 5–6.

House of Bishops of the General Synod, *Protecting All God's Children*, Church House Publishing, 2004.

Reginald Johnson, *Your Personality and the Spiritual Life*, Monarch, 1995.

Fremont Kast and James Rosenzweig, *Management of Systems: A Contingency Approach*, McGraw Hill, 1985.

Ian P. McGreal (ed.), *Great Thinkers of the Eastern World*, HarperCollins, 1995.

Anthony de Mello SJ, *Sadhana – A Way to God. Christian Exercises in Eastern Form*, Doubleday, 1978.

Diarmuid O'Murchu, *Reclaiming Spirituality – A New Spiritual Framework for Today's World*, Gill & Macmillan, 1997.

S. Radhakrishnan, *The Bhagvadgita*, HarperCollins, 1993.

Carl Rogers, *On Becoming a Person*, Houghton Muffin, 1961.

Carl Rogers, *A Way of Being*, Houghton Muffin, 1980.

*The Shorter Oxford English Dictionary*, 3rd edn, Oxford University Press, 1973.

Gordon S. Wakefield (ed.), *A Dictionary of Christian Spirituality*, SCM Press, 1983.

Hans-Rudi Weber, *Experiments with Bible Study*, World Council of Churches, 1981.

John White, *Changing on the Inside – The Keys to Spiritual Recovery and Lasting Change*, Eagle, 1991.

William Whyte, *The Organisation Man*, Penguin, 1960; first published by Simon & Schuster, 1956.

Theodore Zeldin, 'An intimate history of conversation', in BBC *Education*, 22 March 1998.